You Will Make It Through

Ed Taylor

You Will Make It Through

By: Ed Taylor

Copyright © 2020 by Ed Taylor

ISBN: 978-0-9965723-0-9

All Scripture quotations, unless otherwise noted, are taken from the New King James Version ®. Copyright © 1982 by Thomas Nelson, Inc. Used by permission. All rights reserved.

Abounding Grace Media
18900 E. HAMPDEN AVE. AURORA, CO 80013
(303) 628-7200

Who wants to be in a crisis? I don't, and I'm sure you n't. I am positive that your neighbor doesn't. And yet, ses come to us all. We face big ones. We face little ones. face temporary ones, and we face long ones. If there is thing that we all share, it's definitely the common pain suffering. With the latest challenges in our world ught on by the global pandemic, things have gotten far rse. On top of the daily struggles, issues, and ongoing llenges, now you are faced with additional pressures rywhere around you. I'm sure it's been a constant battle stay strong, stay committed, and stay clear-headed as u follow Jesus. It feels like you're on your heels, always easy. Your life may even feel unstable.

re's the good news- you are not alone. God is with you. has promised to never leave you or forsake you. Those promises to build your life on. Promises that we need keep at the forefront of our minds continually.

e Bible is full of men and women who faced great, urmountable challenges and came out victorious.

"And what more shall I say? For the time would fail me ell of Gideon and Barak and Samson and Jephthah, also of vid and Samuel and the prophets: who through faith, dued kingdoms, worked righteousness, obtained promises, pped the mouths of lions, quenched the violence of fire,

escaped the edge of the sword, out of weakness were ma
strong, became valiant in battle, turned to flight the armies of
aliens. Women received their dead raised to life again. Oth
were tortured, not accepting deliverance, that they might obt
a better resurrection. Still others had trial of mockings a
scourgings, yes, and of chains and imprisonment. They w
stoned, they were sawn in two, were tempted, were slain w
the sword. They wandered about in sheepskins and goatski
being destitute, afflicted, tormented—of whom the world w
not worthy. They wandered in deserts and mountains, in d
and caves of the earth. And all these, having obtained a go
testimony through faith, did not receive the promise, C
having provided something better for us, that they should
be made perfect apart from us." Hebrews 11:32–40 (NKJV)

Don't think for a moment that the men and women of t
Bible are better than you. They, too, were real people livi
real lives and facing real problems trusting in a real Go
They were able to make it! You too will make it –by fai
God will enable you to make it through your present tri

Really? Yes, you read that right, you are going to make
through. I'm sure you're thinking, "I don't want to make
THROUGH the trial; I want to be taken **OUT** of the tria
Me, too. I don't want to go through a trial any more th
you do. But that's life. We all face and go through tria

d many of them take a long time exacting a heavy toll on
r lives.

ere are those times when God does a tremendous work
our lives, and He does indeed deliver us "**FROM**" the
al. It's over. It's in the past. We can rejoice that we made
out! Yet, more often than not, we are being delivered
HROUGH" the trial. When Jesus says we are going to
e other side, you can be sure, no matter what we face
ng the way, we will make it to the other side!

"Now it happened, on a certain day, that He got into a
at with His disciples. And He said to them, "Let us cross over
he other side of the lake." And they launched out." Luke 8:22
KJV)

e work of God in and through us comes as we daily live
th the difficulties. The Spirit of God is burning deep into
r hearts the very character of Jesus. He is developing
thin us the very essence of perseverance.

e don't use the word perseverance too much these days.
tead, we use words like patience, determination, or
ybe resolve. But the Bible word is a powerful one and
rth taking a look at more in-depth. It's an interesting
rd that is typically used in direct connection with trials.

Sometimes it's translated as "perseverance":

And not only that but we also glory in tribulatio[n] knowing that tribulation produces perseverance; a[nd] perseverance, character; and character, hope. Now hope do[es] not disappoint, because the love of God has been poured out [in] our hearts by the Holy Spirit who was given to us. Romans 5[:]5 (NKJV)

Other times it's translated "endurance":

"Therefore we also, since we are surrounded by so gr[eat] a cloud of witnesses, let us lay aside every weight, and the [sin] which so easily ensnares us, and let us run with endurance [the] race that is set before us…." Hebrews 12:1 (NKJV)

The word comes from the Greek word "hupomone" a[nd] literally means to "bear up under, patience, endura[nce] toward things or circumstances." It speaks of a constan[cy] and continuation under suffering with faith and duty. T[he] call of God is to wait upon Him, and to trust Him, to clea[ve] to Him, to endure what you're facing. Each time th[e] encouragement comes, we can remember that God [is] cheering you on, encouraging you and me not to quit! I w[ill] say that again: don't quit! What you will lose throu[gh] quitting is far worse than the trial you're facing!

rseverance is at the center of your life as a believer. It's urs already given to you as a gift from God. He is inside you, strengthening you to not cave in and quit, so that u won't fall to the schemes and wickedness of the enemy, not run away motivated by fear. As the author of the brews said, "you have need of endurance." God Himself ets that need! We are able to live with His strength as trust Him by faith!

en this world knows what it's like to stay strong in the dst of difficulty. Winston Churchill is quoted as saying, ever give in, never give in, never, never, never, in thing, great or small, large or petty, never give in except convictions of honor and good sense. Never give in." at stirring words! But in and of themselves, those words ve absolutely no spiritual power!

u are a believer in Jesus Christ! He gives you the nmand and the power! The secret of our day-by-day, ment-by-moment victory is to surrender. To surrender r will, emotions, and lives to Jesus daily, abiding in Him. e choose to endure the trial, knowing that God has a rpose in it all!

e of the keys to endurance is the need for us to look unto us. This mindset is so good. Where our eyes are looking, ere our focus is crisp, where our attention is drawn affects every aspect of our lives! The need of looking up Jesus is absolute.

> Therefore we also, since we are surrounded by so grea cloud of witnesses, let us lay aside every weight, and the which so easily ensnares us, and let us run with endurance race that is set before us, looking unto Jesus, the author a finisher of our faith. Who for the joy that was set before H endured the cross, despising the shame, and has sat down at right hand of the throne of God. Hebrews 12:1-2 (NKJV)

We should be doing that every day. It will greatly help y make it to the other side of your trial!

The word translated "looking" in the original Gre language is rich and beautiful. The only time we see it us is in the New Testament. It's a word which means to "lc steadfastly" or "fix your mind upon." It means that you ta your attention off of everything else around you a gazing intently, looking unto Jesus!

Think for a moment of all the things that so easily take yo eyes off of Jesus: money, relationships, sports, retireme houses, cars, social media, and yes, trials! Some of the things can block out our view of Jesus so much that become blind to His goodness and love for us! But there a race of faith you and I are running. Your life matters to

ny! This race isn't a sprint, as if it would be over so
.ckly. It's a lifelong pace focused upon the Lord! We
ist make a determined decision to yield ourselves to the
ly Spirit, choosing to "look unto Jesus," focused intently
Him.

us is the supreme example of our faith! He is the Author,
Originator, Pioneer, the One who begins and takes the
d. He originated all of the faith that we read about in the
le and lived and experienced it firsthand! Jesus is the
ef Leader and example for us! He lived the supreme life
faith! Jesus is also the Finisher, the One who carries
ough to completion. Jesus cried out loudly from the
ss, "**IT IS FINISHED!**" It is, friend! We know that what
us starts, He finishes. And He's not done with you yet.

"For your fellowship in the gospel from the first day until
v, being confident of this very thing, that He who has begun
>od work in you will complete it until the day of Jesus Christ;"
lippians 1:5–6 (NKJV)

re we are running our race, and it's getting harder. Trials
>und. Isolation is harsh. Loneliness is deafening, and
're ready to give up. It even seems like it would be easier
throw in the towel. NO! It's time to get our eyes back on
us. Get back into His Word and read the Bible every day.

11

Get back into a regular rhythm of prayer and talk to Hi
every day.

The moment you choose to look unto Jesus, things get
much clearer. You remember that He loves you. He di
for you. He rose again the third day to prove th
everything He said is true. He is ready to strengthen y
and help you along the way! He started something in yo
life when you were born again. He will complete it. I
endured. I can endure. Yes! The shame, the humiliatio
the pain, the beatings didn't slow Jesus down one bit! I
endured all the way to the end!

But why? Why is this happening? Why me? Why did G
allow this painful situation to come into my life? I lo
Him, and I serve Him. I don't want it! I'm sorry, frier
indeed, it IS painful. It is hard. It is challenging.

Often in our lives, we face problems, circumstanc
hardships, sorrows, sufferings, trials, and then we ask t
same question. I must have asked it a thousand times! I
asked out of a sincere heart and desire, I know. But it
often makes things worse for us because God does
always reveal the reasons for why He is allowing things
exactly what He is doing behind the scenes.

"For My thoughts are not your thoughts, Nor are your ways My ways," says the LORD. "For as the heavens are higher than the earth, So are My ways higher than your ways, And My thoughts than your thoughts." Isaiah 55:8–9 (NKJV)

Here's the thing to remember; God knows all things. He knows everything that there is to know! God has the advantage of omniscience. Remember, the Bible tells us that God knows all things from the beginning. Every decision that He makes is right, true, and just. It's so different for you and me, isn't it? When we make decisions, we don't have all the information or all of the facts or even know what is happening in the spiritual realm (unless the Lord reveals it to us). We make our decisions by faith. When God makes a decision, He never makes a mistake. He knows why you're facing what you're facing. He knows. You can trust Him.

We spend so much time chasing after an answer to the "why" question that our faith dwindles, and our lives get worse, not better! The right response to trials in our lives is faith. We are learning how to trust God. He knows, and because of Him, you will make it through this difficulty.

Why does God allow the things that He allows? I don't know. But He does. It's important to remember that God has not promised an easy life to any of us. The Bible teaches

the exact opposite; life will be harder in many wa
following Jesus Christ. They hated Him and killed hi
Jesus reminded us that because they hated Him, they w
hate us also.

"These things I have spoken to you, that in Me you m
have peace. In the world you will have tribulation; but be
good cheer, I have overcome the world." John 16:33 (NKJV)

"Strengthening the souls of the disciples, exhorting th
to continue in the faith, and saying, "We must through ma
tribulations enter the kingdom of God." Acts 14:22 (NKJV)

"Yes, and all who desire to live godly in Christ Jesus w
suffer persecution." 2 Timothy 3:12 (NKJV)

"I, John, both your brother and companion in
tribulation and kingdom and patience of Jesus Christ, was on
island that is called Patmos for the word of God and for
testimony of Jesus Christ." Revelation 1:9 (NKJV)

Why then does God allow the suffering, the pain,
persecution, and the hardships? We don't know becau
God doesn't give us the answer. He doesn't expl
Himself to us.

e fact is, there are many things that we simply don't
ow.

times like this we must discipline ourselves to
member and think upon those things that we do know
sure.

e know God is love:

"Beloved, let us love one another, for love is of God; and
eryone who loves is born of God and knows God. He who
es not love does not know God, for God is love." 1 John 4:7-8
KJV)

e know God loves you, supremely:

"The thief does not come except to steal, and to kill, and
destroy. I have come that they may have life, and that they
y have it more abundantly." John 10:10 (NKJV)

**e know God so loved you that He gave His only
gotten Son for you:**

"For God so loved the world that He gave His only
gotten Son, that whoever believes in Him should not perish
have everlasting life." John 3:16 (NKJV)

We know God is sovereign, and nothing happens that He hasn't allowed:

"Are not two sparrows sold for a copper coin? And no one of them falls to the ground apart from your Father's will. But the very hairs of your head are all numbered. Do not fear therefore; you are of more value than many sparrows." Matt 10:29-31 (NKJV)

We know God's thoughts toward you are good and not evil, for a future and a hope:

"For I know the thoughts that I think toward you, says the LORD, thoughts of peace and not of evil, to give you a future and a hope." Jeremiah 29:11 (NKJV)

We know God is working out His eternal plan for your life:

"The LORD will perfect that which concerns me; Your mercy, O LORD, endures forever; Do not forsake the works of Your hands." Psalm 138:8 (NKJV)

We know God is working with eternity in view, not just the temporary:

"But the end of all things is at hand; therefore be serious and watchful in your prayers. And above all things have fervent love for one another, for "love will cover a multitude of sins." hospitable to one another without grumbling. As each one eived a gift, minister it to one another, as good stewards of manifold grace of God. If anyone speaks, let him speak as the cles of God. If anyone ministers, let him do it as with the lity which God supplies, that in all things God may be rified through Jesus Christ, to whom belong the glory and the minion forever and ever. Amen." 1 Peter 4:7-11 (NKJV)

know that our present sufferings are nothing mpared with the glory that will be revealed in us:

"For I consider that the sufferings of this present time are worthy to be compared with the glory which shall be ealed in us." Romans 8:18 (NKJV)

hen you face problems and situations like you are right w, that you simply don't understand, and when rything seems to be going wrong and the pain seems bearable, like it will never end, it's vital to shift back ur thinking to the things that you know for sure.

at about the "why" question? The answer comes in mitting and trusting ourselves to God's loving care. Bible instructs us to live a life of ever-increasing faith. r thoughts, our feelings, our understanding, and our lanations are not to be trusted! Only the Word of God o be trusted. He is faithful to keep His Word!

"Trust in the LORD with all your heart And lean not [on] your own understanding; In all your ways acknowledge H[im], And He shall direct your paths. Do not be wise in your own e[yes;] Fear the LORD and depart from evil. It will be health to y[our] flesh, And strength to your bones." Proverbs 3:5–8 (NKJV)

We go through heavy experiences in life. We go throu[gh] suffering. We go through intense pain. We do[n't] understand why God in His love would allow us to su[ffer] like this, but we trust Him. He's working out His eter[nal] purposes in our lives. His plan for our lives is better tha[n a] thousand plans that we could ever dream up.

No, we don't know the reasons why today. No, we do[n't] understand it all right. Even so, we choose to trust God [and] wait for Him to reveal to us what exactly He is doing.

Looking back on my own life, many things happened to [me] that were painful and confusing. I've experien[ced] hardship, pain, and unbearable grief. I have also beg[ged] God for an answer, explanation, or a reason- and hea[ven] was silent. God didn't explain Himself to me. Friend, [as I] look back now on some of those same trials, I can see n[ow] more clearly what God was doing in that season of my [life.] Wow, that was it! Even so, there are many things whe[re I] still have no idea what God is doing.

learning to fall back on what I do know about God. He
es me; God is faithful. He is truly my strength, and He
ed my life. God is good; He is watching out for me.
o, He is working all things together for my good and
glory.

n learning that knowing "why" is not as important as
wing "Who." I choose to look to Him. I don't have to
e every question answered in my life related to my
ls and setbacks. What is important is that I just trust in
n and commit my ways to Him. As I learn to accept my
, I can rest. I can trust God because I know He knows
at He's doing in my life. I commit my ways to Him, and
rest is mine by faith. I can enjoy a perfect peace because
mind is focused on Him!

"You will keep him in perfect peace, Whose mind is
ed on You, Because he trusts in You. Trust in the LORD
ver, For in YAH, the LORD, is everlasting strength." Isaiah
–4 (NKJV)

proper response to trials and troubles, pain, and
blems, is an internal choice to continue forward in the
d by faith. As painful as it is in your life right now, it's
l you take the next step forward in your life. It's
ortant for you to do the next thing by faith. Times of
at trial and temptations are not the time to quit. *Please*

don't quit. What you'd lose because of quitting is far greater t[...]
you could ever know.

It's true that the calling of the believer is to a life of p[...]
and problems. Some mistakenly thought or were wron[...]
taught, that their new life in Christ would be one[...]
continual happiness free from pain. The exact opposit[...]
true. The believer's life is filled with all of the problem[...]
living in a fallen world, plus the new spiritual challen[...]
that come from following Jesus. Jesus promised that in [...]
world, we would experience tribulations.

"These things I have spoken to you, that in Me you [...]
have peace. In the world you will have tribulation; but b[...]
good cheer, I have overcome the world." John 16:33 (NKJV)

Paul was warned of the "many" things he would suffer[...]
the name of Christ!

"But the Lord said to him, "Go, for he is a chosen ve[...]
of Mine to bear My name before Gentiles, kings, and the chil[...]
of Israel. For I will show him how many things he must su[...]
for My name's sake." Acts 9:15–16 (NKJV)

If you try to sidestep this truth, you are trying to sides[...]
the will of God. Don't be surprised or shocked that tr[...]

re increased in your life. It's part of the normal Christian
perience.

.

"Beloved, do not think it strange concerning the fiery trial
ich is to try you, as though some strange thing happened to
u; but rejoice to the extent that you partake of Christ's
ferings, that when His glory is revealed, you may also be glad
h exceeding joy." 1 Peter 4:12–13 (NKJV)

netimes we think we are the only ones going through
ficult times. In some ways, it is true. You have a
queness about you, and the trial you're currently in has
que ingredients that make it super hard for you but not
essarily others around you. Don't ever forget: you're not
ne. Suffering is shared by everyone, and suffering in the
urch of Jesus Christ has been with us from the very first
r it was started. Throughout the book of Acts, followers
Jesus have met with dreadful opposition, painful
oression, governmental wickedness, and a whole host of
l and nefarious plots to destroy lives and crush the
urch's very existence. The goal was to wipe the church
the planet. Yet the Church valiantly met every attack,
ry pain, every suffering, and survived. In many ways,
Church has thrived under the attempts to harm and
troy Her! Why is this important to remember? Because
are the Church. You, too, will survive. You, too, will
ve! God is always using what you're going through for

His eternal purposes. What you're facing today will destroy you. You will make it through! This diffi season in your life is an opportunity to re-align your with the Lord.

As the early church grew and faced many different tri the believers were encouraged to "continue" at least th times. That's the answer to your trial, too. Contir Continue on. Continue worshipping Jesus. Conti forward. Three times in the book of Acts, we find believers encouraged to continue.

The first time is in Acts 11:23 where the believers w encouraged to "continue with the Lord". Oh, how we n to be speaking more about the Lord when difficult tir come. As tough and challenging situations increase a grow, we too want to talk about, think about, and sh more about the Lord than ever!

"Then news of these things came to the ears of the chu in Jerusalem, and they sent out Barnabas to go as far as Antic When he came and had seen the grace of God, he was glad, encouraged them all that with purpose of heart they shc continue with the Lord." Acts 11:22–23 (NKJV)

The second time is in Acts 13:43 where believers w encouraged to "continue in the grace of God." Oh, how

st remember God's gracious love toward us in tough
es. Hard times are not intended to get more work out of
more effort, more activity, but rather God is
ouraging us to continue to rest in the grace of God. This
l help guard you from becoming so unloving and
;racious because you're hurting. Remember, hurting
»ple tend to hurt people. Continuing in the grace of God
l help you be more gracious!

"Now when the congregation had broken up, many of
Jews and devout proselytes followed Paul and Barnabas,
», speaking to them, persuaded them to continue in the grace
;od." Acts 13:43 (NKJV)

 third time is in Acts 14:21-22, where the believers are
orted to "continue in the faith." We know that without
h, it's impossible to please God. We don't throw away
 trust in the Lord just because it's hard. No! We ask for
re faith. We exercise what little faith we have to cling to
Lord. We press in even more. We hold on to faith. We
ose not to let go!

"And when they had preached the gospel to that city and
le many disciples, they returned to Lystra, Iconium, and
ioch, strengthening the souls of the disciples, exhorting them
ontinue in the faith, and saying, "We must through many
ulations enter the kingdom of God." Acts 14:21–22 (NKJV)

You read that right; tribulations are normal. This i
continual theme throughout the Bible. Troubles await
and me—many of them. Yet once again, we are encoura
that we will get "THROUGH" them. Yes, we go throt
them. We pass through them. We will get through them

We all need the reminder that God is faithful even wl
we are hurting and under great spiritual oppression. H
we respond makes all the difference in the world.

Just before the Church received this import
encouragement in Acts 14, Paul endured a hea
debilitating trial. He was literally stoned half to death.
people became so mad and angry with him that they li
up heavy stones and thrust them upon Paul's body, to
point where they thought they were successful in kill
him. Then they dragged his lifeless body out to the tr
heap. If ever there was a time where Paul could throv
the towel with good reason, it would have been tl
"Enough is enough," would have been a normal ratic
thought. But Paul was strengthened by the Lord. The B
says He "rose up" and went right back into the city
preach the gospel. Did you hear that? The worst happe:
to him, and he chose to get up and go back into the cit'
share God's love. He didn't quit.

"Then Jews from Antioch and Iconium came there; and
ʳing persuaded the multitudes, they stoned Paul and dragged
ₕ out of the city, supposing him to be dead. However, when
disciples gathered around him, he rose up and went into the
ʳ. And the next day he departed with Barnabas to Derbe."
s 14:19–20 (NKJV)

u, too, need to get up and go forward. You can do it in
strength of the Lord. Get up. Make the decision right
w and then do it. He is with you.

e the believers in Acts 11, the greatest choice we can
ke is to purpose in our hearts to continue with the Lord.
akes a real purpose of heart to live the Christian life
en we find opposition at every turn.

u are opposed by the world, and its secular, anti-God
ture. The world is hostile to the Church. Never will the
rld and its systems approve of God or His children (1
n 2:15).

u are opposed by your flesh, constantly, continually. It's
attle moment by moment to just do the right thing
latians 5:17).

You are opposed by the devil and demonic realm. works together with the world to provoke your flesh, a then watches the destruction follow (1 Peter 5:8).

Living the life of a Christian is so much more than a simp emotional decision. It is more than just making up y mind to follow Jesus. You must be born again. As a n creation in Christ, empowered and indwelt by the Spiri God, you then purpose in your heart to continue. Mak progress in tough times requires that you make a purpo commitment of surrender. Daniel is a great example of t in Daniel Chapter 1. Under unreal pressure, Daniel mac decision in his heart. It was internal, personal, a powerful. It is what is required of you, too. Purpose in y heart to ignore the noise and continue with the Lord.

I know it's easy to get angry, frustrated, and even bi during difficult times. Those are not the proper respon: They will only hurt you deeply and defile those closes you. Opposition and pain are normal. Expect it a continue in the Lord!

The exhortation to continue with the Lord is needed. M. people start the Christian walk with great zeal and fer and excitement. But as time goes on, their love for things of God grows cold. Eventually, it ends with th departing from the faith. You don't want your current p d heartache to cause that to happen to you! fortunately, as a pastor, I see it happen all the time. It's vays heartbreaking to watch.

important that you cling to the Lord through this trial, end. In the Old King James Version of the Bible, they nslated the word "continue" as the word "cleave." Isn't t such a cool word? It means to "hang on", "stay close", "remain strong." When a couple gets married, we mind them that God's will is for them to "leave their ther and father and cleave to one another." They are to ntinue together forever! So, too, you are to leave the ughts of quitting and cleave to the Lord. *Continue on h Him, in His grace, by faith!* Don't let anything courage you from sticking close to Him. The world will ke fun of you and assault you. Your flesh will scream you to quit at every turn. The devil will be there to ploit your weaknesses and plant doubts in your mind.

n't ever leave His side. You will make it through. You d the strength that He gives, and the help He provides. everlasting presence to comfort and establish you.

is loves you, and He is with you. You will make it ough this. We will make it through together!

Connect with Ed Taylor
Mail: c/o Calvary Church
18900 E. Hampden Ave.
Aurora, CO 80013
Phone: 303-628-7200

Websites:
edtaylor.org
calvaryco.church
Email: ed@edtaylor.org